LIFE

WHITE LAVENDER

I dedicate my work to life and my loved ones.

Life teaches us about everything and nothing, it gives us the means to be.

Our loved ones teach us about everything and nothing too, they make our life full of emotions, they give us reasons to feel and experience those different emotions, they are with us all the time in our hearts and share their love for us in their own ways, be it small or big.

I dedicate this book to all of them who have given me the reason to exist, and to those too who gave me the means to exist.

Contents

Contents

Preface

The journey of our life is special in its own way and is worth every bit of pain we suffer at the end of it.

I wrote this book of poems because for me it was a method of sharing and showing everyone my work.

My friends and family encouraged me to write more and told me that when spent effort my work can be rather good so I chose such platform to showcase it and share it.

I personally hope that all my readers like them as much as I myself along with my friends and close ones liked.

1. Pride Is Our Hearts Cure

Peak out of the closet

Or barge out

It is your posit

Whether you whisper or shout

Ignore the chit-chat around you

People will always judge

It's your choice how in the future you grow

What's your idea for a celebration including some fudge?

No matter whom you like

Be it a girl or a guy

It will surely come out, as the truth always strikes

Ignore the whispers

As they tend to flow

Don't let it ruffle your whiskers

And make your progress slow

Step ahead

And make your move

Don't let fear in your head make its bed

And grow into a grove

The choice is yours

Don't let others interfere
Content is the cure
And our happiness's chosen care
Life is an adventurous ride
Which happens to be on the side of the wild
Who thinks death is not right
Happens to be not as bright.

2. A Flower For My Soulmate

The soft pinkish hue

Has gathered some dew

Reflecting the sun

Having some fun

Lying in a patch of green

Breathing in air clean

Softer than silk

Smoother than milk

Waiting for you

Under the sky blue

Topped with fairy dust

Free of any rust

Waiting for you

In the middle of ocean blue

Placed with love

By the dove

Watered by nature

Grown by nomenclature

Free of any hate

Only for you my soulmate.

3. Breaths Worth

With every breath I took
Inside me, my heart shook
Helping me survive
While some other lost their lives
Is it selfish to continue to live a bit more
When others have pain left to endure.

4. Broken Trust

I placed my trust in you
And you broke it out of the blue
The feeling of betrayal filled my vein
Flowing around searching for any and every drain
Finding none, it continues to flow around
Basing it on my reasonings ground
At first, it made me depressed
But time finally made it to be suppressed
After my life's sunset
Accompanied by pillows teary wet
Came my fresh sunrise
Follow by the entry of my best friend who happened to be very
wise
I got what I needed
A new start which was not beaded
With fresh air in my blood
It was happiness with which my life had a flood
So, I say to you
Don't show me your face
Even out of the blue
As my life isn't a race
To win

By you are your kin
I am not shy
But this is the final bye.

5. New start – Old cycle

Sorry sweet heart
I am not in love with you
Now the time has come for a new start
As my new life is across the ocean blue
Across the winds ranged blow
With the oceans flow
Swimming in the emotional well
Yeh! No time dwell.

6. Life of a Tree

As the wind blowed
I saw it had glowed
Be it from happiness
Or from the rays reflectiveness
But what I do know
Is that on the time unknown
There will come a day
When it will decay
Completing it's own cycle of life
Without ever using a knife.

7. Farmer's Work

With time they grow
From being nurtured as a seed
To being reaped when time
Turning dust to gold (in its worth)
All the way to calming the monsters of hunger
With the ups and downs
And cold and warm
Never giving up on its path to heaven
Jumping, rolling, tumbling, drolling
Only a farmer knows what to sow
Playing with mud and shaping it at his heart's desire
Hiding the seeds in the depth of mother's womb
Peddling the cycle of life
Be it his or the seeds.

8. Ever Wondered?

Have you ever wondered,
What lies in the void of nothingness?
What grows in the womb of Darkness?
What hides behind the sparkles of light?
Waiting for you to arrive.

9. Mastermind

Growing in the shadows
Stronger they became
Step by step
Games they played
Dancing they went
As the hours were turned
Twisting and turning
Unseen they remained
Situations arised and they were seen as kind
But when looked deeper and deeper enough
They were the mastermind.

10. The Mega Drive

With the speed of lightning
The moments do change
But we only feel it
When we are in the impactful range
Beware of your steps
Or you will fall
Tumbling and dumbling
Into the great hall
On reaching there the jokers will arrive
Making you participate in the mega drive
Then you will be in for a ride
Over a mountain dried
From there you will be sliding down
Riding a mopping clown
Then comes eating a mountain of pie
Hoping you won't die
If you were to still survive
You will win the mega drive.

11. Crows and Petals

With the blow of wind
The petals will fall
Marking the change of seasons
With a celebratory ball
Hearts will soar
Love will be more
Bees will dance
Bears will take a chance
Plants will grow
There goes a crow
Looking for his food
Hunger is his mood
Down the lane
Into the haunted house
Flying like a plane
Hiding like a mouse
Searching for food to pick
Gliding into fog thick
From the way he goes
On the sight of his target he slows.

12. Headless man's simple day

Crackling like fire
In the night as dire
Goes a headless man
Riding a white van
Roaming in every corner
Lost like a foreigner
Crying like a kiddow
Swinging in the meadow
Looking in the fire
Missing his sire
Sat there he
Drinking his tea.

13. A Shopping Trip

If you trip from a tree
It can't stop you from a shopping spree
Round and round you go
Trying new dresses you show
Compassion or not
Found any dress to be bought
Sliding you go on the tile
Walking down the ramp with style
Sucking on an ice pop
Remember to pay the bill for the shop
Up and down the floor
In search of dresses more
Dresses pink, blue, or red
It's the bill you truly dread
Hands filled with bags
It's you who had them snagged
End approaches as you reach your house
Little bags filled with broches to be wrapped
As a gift from a certain santa clause.

14. A Close Call

Shy little girl
Stepping on the stone
Petting the dog
Who is looking for a bone
Jumping through the river
Sending the water into shiver
Goes there she
Looking for a bee
When came across a hive
Had to take a big dive
Into the river nearby
As the bee turned out not a bit shy
Looking around
Crawling on the ground
Went there she
Hiding from the enraged bee
When reached her home
Quickly hid in her dome.

15. Rubbles Life Bubble

Tip-toeing along the line
Goes there a friend of mine
Rubble is his name
Trouble is his passion
A good laugh is his aim
Complex is his situation
On the hill
Behind the mill
Lives there he
Along with me
Jumping on his paws
While swiping his claws
There he goes
Wearing some bows
Sniffing the bud
Shaking the mud
Barking out loud
Towards the black cloud
Running towards his home
With all his might
For a before the sleep comb
And barking his good night.

16. Break The Cage to the Wide World

Play with the world
All over the page
Fly like some bird
Don't sit in the cage
Maybe it's made of gold
But that doesn't make you bold
Walk out of the cage you built
But be careful or you will be killed
The world out there is waiting for you
You will do good remembring not everything is green and blue
It happens to be very wide
And its the same place where many had died
Don't let your talent be supressed
Or the result will surely make you depressed
The competition out there is very tight
So I say that fight with all your might.

17. Lifes a Challenge

Not your sweetu types

Make sure you carry some of those wet wipes

Looks or not it ain't easy

Those emotions make me queasy

Use your mouth when needed

Not all your dresses are beaded

Become the flower grown on a cactus

But don't you dare disturb us

As you surely won't like the attention on you

And I guarantee that no one will wanna be in your shoe

Those self-proclaimed heroes won't last

Soon they will only be a thing of past

If you wanna do something then do something big

Or you will be just a laughing stock for people to take a dig

Take a few zig-zags and shake your bum

Sitting here will only make you dumb

Make sure all your enemies are in your sight

As it will make it easy to fight

Don't you dare back down

As I promise it will turn you into a clown.

18. Natures Watery Diamond

While watching the rain
A thought came into my brain
About how the water glows
When it freely flows
In and out of the valley
In its own rally
Helping everyone in need
Without a single drop of greed.

19. Mindless Wonder

With the tick of the world
And tock of the word
One would wonder when the silencle would come
And if our live would stop beating like a drum
One would wonder
When our life stop being a blunder
Would we live long enough for the day
Or would our mind decay.

20. Water-Water What Are You

Water is a mystery
With its own history
No knowledge of where it comes
I wonder if its heaven from where it dumps
With crystals coolness
And a saint's afoolness
It flows all around
Like the path of a merry-go-round
I wonder what's inside you
And if you truly are reflecting the colour blue
What do you truly taste like
And how much of you is waste like
You will always be a mystery to me
And its to be seen if there is any future for us to see.

21. Small Wonders Of Life

When I walked in there
While doing my hair
The aroma I smelt
Made my heart melt
Taking in a whiff of it
Watching the treat, laying there to be bit
To take a piece of cake
I had to wait for it to bake
And when it was done
I felt giddy, at the mere thought of eating it
And oh! What fun it was! What fun!
As it made my face lit
Out of happiness due to the taste
Savouring every bit, as not to make it waste.

22. In The Valleys Of Shilong

While watching the sky of the night
My eyes fell upon the stars shining beautifully bright
Covered by mist and cloud
Ignoring the people who are very loud
It seems to be filled with diamonds
Which can shine without any help from the almonds
Lying on crispy green grass
Watching the stars through a telescope made of brass
Ignoring everyone around
Searching for something which happens to be nowhere near
found
With the company of my friend butterfly
Who is telling me an utter lie
It said that the stars contains wrinkles
And that's why they twinkle
Then it flew away to suck the nectar from a flower
While I waited for a meteor shower
All night long
In the valley of Shilong.

23. Memories Of Life

Watching the sea
Reminded me
Of the time we spent
Sitting beside the tent
In the middle of the forest
With you and our darling florist
Whom we lost on the way
With the enemy he had to slay.

24. Life-Afterlife

While your smile happens to be very sweet
I still prefer the bird's tweet
Out in the nature
Free of the society's nomenclature
No one to gossip about you
Roaming around without any clue
Free of the world's burden
After my death which was really sudden
I crossed the life's veil
And sat on the afterlife's rail
Eating ice cream of flavor unknown
In a chocolate-covered cone
Crossing the bridge
Which is kind of a ridge
I went on my way
To form a new life with some clay.

25. The Creator's Craft

While reading the letter
I thought of the creator
Who made us
Without a single fuss
Knowing our nature
Which is similar to whom we call a creature
They didn't even bat an eye
Told us that one day we will all die
Told us to do whatever we want to do
But be careful as not to do something we would regret in the end
too
The love we felt
Made our heart melt
Making us faithful to them
With every inch of our stem
Without even knowing it
But making us serve them bit by bit
With or without a strife.

26. Fight for right

I don't write for the sake of writing
But for my hearts desire
I won't be ashamed for fighting
If it's to save my passion's fire
One should never back down
If they think what they are doing is right
Even if people frown
At your mere sight
Don't care if people call a fued
As at the end its them who are to get rued
No need to have a fright
As the truth will always strick
Charge ahead
The mighty never truly falls
You might be scared but the truth is not to be dread
It's what you worked hard for and that takes some balls
You deserve to be praised
As you have done the right
Make sure the voices are raised
When something wrong catches your sight
Past is not a thing to dwell
But a source from where we learn

WHITE LAVENDER

Don't let it's burden swell
As it won't give you a turn.

27. A New But Familiar Glow

By flowing in this overly familiar row
My heart has started to glow
Now that I finally have it
I realize that this is what I always wanted as a kid
To be cherished and have someone to love
Be it from my close ones or in form of a dove.

28. Preening-Green

Looking into your eyes green
Reminded me of how you preen
Admiring those smooth wavey hair
Oh my! It's not fair
Others look towards you in jealousy
But I know you are a delicacy
Which belongs to no one but you
And everyone should get a clear clue
If it were up to me
Then I won't let you go out of my eyes for others to see
But I won't, as it's very rude
And I don't wanna come as crude
My intentions towards you are to protect
And I beg you not to reject
May you have a good life ahead of you
And nothing harms you even out of blue

29. For My Role Model

When I watched you grow
I had raised my eyebrow
As you never did what the society told
And when questioned, you did not fold
You showed courage unlike any
And became the inspiration to many
To become a role model like you is my desire
And for that, I have to make sure no one extinguishes the fire
In your own way
Becoming an inspirational ray
For many to come and go
And to not become a road-side show
You did what you thought was right
And ended up with a future bright
In the end, you succeeded
Without your face turning tomato red.

30. Her

When the snow began to fall
She came and dressed me like a doll
When I fell to the ground due to a puddle
She came around and stayed with me to cuddle
When I wasn't bold
Due to the cold
She came and gave me a hug
As well as a hot-chocolate filled mug
She cared for me
Even when I fell off the tree
She nursed me to full health
Without even caring about her reducing wealth
She opened to me all her heath
Which happens to be bigger than the world's every shopping
mart
She did all she could even from the crowd
And I promised myself that I will make her proud.

Thank You

I would like to thank whoever read my poems and wish that they liked them enough to continue to read my other poem books too.

I intend to continue my writing journey ahead and would hope my readers will continue reading my work.

If any reviews along with queries or suggestions please share them at

'whitelavender628@gmail.com'

I post some of my quotes and poems on

"i_write_whitelavender" on Instagram,

So do stay tuned there for more materials.